LIBYA'S TERRORIST DESCENT: CAUSES AND SOLUTIONS

HEARING

BEFORE THE

SUBCOMMITTEE ON TERRORISM, NONPROLIFERATION, AND TRADE

OF THE

COMMITTEE ON FOREIGN AFFAIRS HOUSE OF REPRESENTATIVES

ONE HUNDRED FOURTEENTH CONGRESS

SECOND SESSION

SEPTEMBER 27, 2016

Serial No. 114–225

Printed for the use of the Committee on Foreign Affairs

Available via the World Wide Web: http://www.foreignaffairs.house.gov/ or http://www.gpo.gov/fdsys/

U.S. GOVERNMENT PUBLISHING OFFICE

21–676PDF   WASHINGTON : 2016

For sale by the Superintendent of Documents, U.S. Government Publishing Office
Internet: bookstore.gpo.gov   Phone: toll free (866) 512–1800; DC area (202) 512–1800
Fax: (202) 512–2104   Mail: Stop IDCC, Washington, DC 20402–0001

CONTENTS

LIBYA'S TERRORIST DESCENT: CAUSES AND SOLUTIONS

TUESDAY, SEPTEMBER 27, 2016

House of Representatives,
Subcommittee on Terrorism, Nonproliferation, and Trade,
Committee on Foreign Affairs,
Washington, DC.

The subcommittee met, pursuant to notice, at 2:15 p.m., in room 2200 Rayburn House Office Building, Hon. Paul Cook presiding.

Mr. Cook. Subcommittee will come to order. Without objection, all members may have 5 days to submit statements, questions and extraneous materials for the record subject to the length limitation in the rules.

Since the U.S.-led NATO intervention in 2011, Libya has completely spiraled out of control and has become a regional and international security threat.

Five years ago, the regime of Libyan dictator Muammar Gaddafi helped us fight against international terrorism. This is not to say that Gaddafi was a good guy. He was a ruthless dictator who sponsored terrorism in the 1980s.

But Gaddafi eventually realized that he was the target of terrorists himself and he changed course to side with us against the cancer of terrorism.

By 2008, U.S. military leaders were calling Libya a top U.S. ally in combating transnational terrorism. Fast forward to today, and Libya is a virtual incubator of terrorist groups, hosting all stripes of jihadi organizations including ISIS and al-Qaeda.

Unfortunately, it was U.S. policy that transformed Libya into the complete failure that it is today. 2011 we decided to intervene in Libya and establish no-fly zones to aid Libyan rebels plotting against Gaddafi.

Under the safety of the no-fly zone we imposed, Islamic terrorist groups long subdued under Gaddafi's regime sprung up, amassed weapons, training and military experience.

Gaddafi was ultimately killed in October 2011. Within days, NATO and U.S. forces packed up and left Libya to its own devices.

It appears that our own Libyan policy at the time was to remove Gaddafi. There was little planning regarding what to do the day after.

Gaddafi's ouster unleashed chaos in the country. Long-simmering political, regional and ethnic divisions suddenly emerged and set Libya on a path toward disaster.

(1)

The country has never recovered. Even the administration says that Libya failed due to our lack of forward thinking. Earlier this year, the President admitted that his administration did not have a plan for post-Gaddafi Libya and he said this was his biggest regret as President.

Dangerous terrorist groups popped up almost immediately to fill the power vacuum created by NATO's intervention. Ansar al-Sharia, al-Qaeda's affiliate in Libya, emerged shortly after Gaddafi's ouster began, deeply entrenching itself in Libya's society by providing social services.

But this did not—this organization did not stop with building schools. They recruited, they armed and trained terrorist fighters intent on carrying out the group's ultimate goal—imposing Islamic law on the country.

These fighters were among those who attacked the U.S. diplomatic compound in Benghazi in 2012, killing Ambassador Christopher Stevens and three of his colleagues.

By 2014, the security situation in Libya had gotten even worse. It became apparent that the country's warring factions were not going to unite anytime soon.

Sensing an opportunity, ISIS announced the establishment of a Libyan affiliate at the end of 2014 and soon began consolidating power around the coast city of Sirte.

From there, ISIS quickly expanded east, west, and south. Terrorists set up checkpoints along the coast and within over a year ISIS managed to hold over 200 kilometers of territory along the Libyan coast.

By the beginning of 2016 reports indicated that ISIS was redirecting recruits and even senior leaders to Libya. It appeared that ISIS was creating what many called a fallback caliphate where it could retreat to in case it was pushed out of Syria and Iraq.

Pentagon estimates suggest the group's ranks in the country quickly swelled to nearly 7,000 fighters. It became apparent that the U.S. needed to target ISIS in Libya as well as in Syria and Iraq.

In August 2016, the U.S. expanded what was until then a very limited air strike campaign with the intention of dislodging the terrorists from their stronghold of Sirte.

By September, the U.S.-backed operation pushed into the last ISIS-held areas of Sirte and freed the city from the reign of terror. But this by no means defeated ISIS in Libya.

Libya remains an ideal foothold for terrorist groups of all kinds and ISIS' removal from Sirte will not be the end of the group. Until we can devise a truly comprehensive long-term strategy to stabilize Libya and defeat the terrorists hiding there, Libya will continue to threaten regional and international security.

Treating the symptoms while ignoring the underlying disease will not solve our problems. ISIS, al-Qaeda, and others will continue to operate at Europe's doorstep and menace the free world. The time has come for America to lead again. Until we do, the world will remain at risk.

I will now turn to the ranking member, Congressman Keating from Massachusetts, for his opening statement.

Mr. KEATING. Thank you, Colonel. I'd like to thank Chairman Poe for calling this hearing and we share a concern for the situation on the ground in Libya and I appreciate the attention we are affording the issue.

I'd also like to thank my colleague, Colonel Cook, for joining us as chair today as well as our panel for joining us to discuss the topic at hand.

The situation in Libya remains very fluid and complex. While the topic of this hearing will focus on the risk or growth of terrorist organizations in the country, I think it's important that we examine the challenges of the interim Libyan government and the lack of a clear strategy from international partners, which contributes to the continued instability.

Since the fall of Gaddafi in 2011, Libya has witnessed pervading and varying levels of instability and civil war resulting from the lack of a strong united government. Libyans and the international community have witnessed a number of interim governments from the General National Congress to the House of Representatives and now, since December of last year, the Government of National Accord—the GNA.

However, the GNA is struggling to build legitimacy and public support in August. The Libyan House of Representatives conducted a vote of no confidence on the new interim government and according to political agreement that created the GNA their House must approve the GNA cabinet before assuming office.

Additionally, the GNA has so far been unable to provide basic services and address long-term issues in Libya such as chronic power and water outages, inflation, a liquidity crisis and a lack of security.

This brings me to the concern today—the rise of ISIL inside the country. As we have seen, since its formation in 2014, ISIL is able to metastasize in places which lack a strong civil society or central government and in Libya the group has managed to establish itself wherever rival militias have not already carved out territories for themselves.

The group has proven capable of launching domestic attacks and Libya's proximity to states such as Tunisia, which struggle with the flow of foreign fighters, make the country an easy destination for extremists.

Fortunately, there has been some success against ISIL by GNA, which has been aided by U.S. air support. In Sirte, for example, anti-ISIL forces have been largely effective in driving out militants from the city.

However, Sirte is just one area and there are still large swaths of land in the south and the west in which ISIL is afforded freedom of movement.

Operation Odyssey Lightning and ISIL's defeat will only succeed as long as GNA is able to capitalize on these security gains and the government's gains.

The question remains what should our role be, that of the United Nations in helping the situation in Libya. I hope during the course of this hearing we examine what can be done both militarily and diplomatically to combat ISIL but also improve their fragile government in Libya.

With that, Mr. Chairman, I'll yield back.

Mr. COOK. Thank you, Congressman Keating.

I now recognize Representative Zeldin from New York for 1 minute.

Mr. ZELDIN. Thank you, Chairman, and I thank all the witnesses who are here for this important hearing. I was recently in Iraq and I had a chance to meet with some of our commanders on the ground.

One interesting observation that was made is that here in the United States we often talk about Iraq, Syria, Libya in that order. The observation that was shared to me is that in many respects we should be talking about Libya, Syria, Iraq, in that order, and the commanders were explaining why—that right now in Iraq we have a strategy to win.

It's tenuous. It can turn. In Syria, my own personal observation—not to put any words into those commanders' mouths is that we seem like maybe we have a strategy to run in place at best as far as Syria goes.

But if we eliminated ISIS from Iraq and even eliminated ISIS from Syria, what I am concerned about is that Libya right now can easily pop up as a new command and control node. So thank you for holding this hearing. It's really important for us to talk about the situation on the ground in Libya.

Mr. COOK. Thank you, Congressman Zeldin.

Congressman Wilson from South Carolina, 1 minute.

Mr. WILSON. Thank you, Mr. Chairman. I appreciate Chairman Ted Poe for convening this timely and important hearing. It is sad that since the fall of Muammar Gaddafi in 2011 a dangerous vacuum has emerged in Libya with numerous, regional and ideological actors competing for power.

Perhaps more dangerously, the past 5 years has given the Islamic State the opportunity to dramatically increase its presence and influence.

I am grateful that recently in August the United States began operation Odyssey Lightning, which is aimed at destroying ISIS along the Libyan coast.

As we have seen throughout its existence, ISIS is a cancer and when it has presence in a country or region there is only oppression and violence. The only way to have a free Libya is the removal of ISIS.

It's important that we have a free and stable government for the people of Libya. I urge promotion of the General National Congress, a foundation for a democratic transition.

I look forward to hearing our witnesses. I yield back.

Mr. COOK. Thank you very much.

By the way, I just got a flash message from Judge Poe. He says Cook, you talk too much, and make sure—by the way, I was going to let you talk for 15 minutes each but he said only keep it 1 minute.

So just to let you know that was not my call. I am only kidding on that, by the way.

Without objection, all of the witnesses' prepared statements will be made part of the record. I ask that each witness please keep your presentation to more—no more than 5 minutes, and I will introduce each witness and then give them time for opening statements.

Dr. Federica Fasanotti—I hope I got that correct—is a non-resident fellow in the Center for 21st Century Security and Intelligence of the foreign policy program of the Brookings Institute.

Her field of work and research have focused on Libya, Afghanistan, Ethiopia, and Somalia. Thank you for joining us.

Mr. Thomas Joscelyn is a senior fellow at the Foundation for Defense of Democracies and senior editor of the Long War Journal, which focuses on counter terrorism and related issues.

Mr. Benjamin Fishman is an adjunct fellow with RAND Corporation's International Security and Defense Policy Center. Previously he served as the Director for North Africa at the National Security Council.

Doctor, we will start with you. You have 5 minutes. Thank you.

STATEMENT OF FEDERICA SAINI FASANOTTI, PH.D., NON-RESIDENT FELLOW, CENTER FOR 21ST CENTURY SECURITY AND INTELLIGENCE, FOREIGN POLICY PROGRAM, THE BROOKINGS INSTITUTION

Ms. FASANOTTI. Okay. Chairman Cook and distinguished members of this committee, thank you for the opportunity to testify today. It's an honor for me to be before you and I'm happy to answer to any question you may have for me after.

Libya's persistent fragmentation is what is most worrying today. Internal divisions are the product of decades of Gaddafi's reckless governing. He played his citizens off of each other and kept them isolated from the rest of the world and also deprived them of any political institution that could keep the country united and stable after he was gone.

Libyan history shows that Libyans have long been divided regionally and locally. Tribes have a long history of fighting one another.

Today, the Libyan state remains immature and those ancient divisions have only gotten worse. At the end of Gaddafi's time in power there were from 100 to 300 armed militia groups. Now there are, according to a European study, about 1,600 militias, gangs and criminal groups.

U.N. Security Council Resolution 1917 put an arms embargo on Libya but today there are more than 20 million weapons circulating in the country of only 6 million people. External powers who have intervened in Libya have actually worsened the polarization and made reconciliation less likely.

It is well known that countries such as Egypt and Emirates have been supporting the toppled government and on the other side Qatar and Turkey did the same with the GNC in Tripoli.

The state of affairs is still going on. Even now that thanks to the UNSMIL mediation in Tripoli, it's been established a Government on National Accord, presumably recognized by most of international actors.

After the 2011 revolution and international intervention, there were few sustainable political options. Social frictions increased in the aftermath of the Gaddafi overthrow and the country's economic fabric eroded.

All these only radicalized the insurgency. The situation in Libya is so compromised that it can be difficult to provide meaningful policy prescriptions.

But I must emphasize that Libya's dramatic downward slide is extremely dangerous for the West and the West should do everything it can to ensure improvement of the situation. In a territory stretching like Alaska are active various shades of Islamic terrorism from the Muslim Brotherhood to al-Qaeda, Ansar al-Sharia, ISIS.

The absence of any state structure has turned the country into an incubator of terrorism ready to act as a trigger for the whole continent.

In the nomadic tradition and experience gained during the Italian domination, handed down from generation to generation, has provided to the Libyans the ability to survive and recover strength even after the heaviest defeats.

In my opinion, there are three key challenges we have to address—the security situation, the severe economic downturn, and deeply fractured politics. These factors are all intertwined and you cannot tackle one if you have not invested in the other.

First, security—Libya is a country at war today. Criminals and their networks are increasingly organized. The state police are powerless even when they exist and the armed forces no longer exists as a coherent entity.

The problem of criminals and militias is connected to the huge amount of weapons. So the first thing to do is try to diminish them.

One policy could be to consider a weapons buyback program which has actually been implemented in Afghanistan in recent years even though in Libya the situations presents many, many different differences.

In the medium term, it is essential that the Libyan armed forces and national security forces and the local police be fundamentally revered.

Second, the economy—before the revolution, Libya's oil-based economy was functional and pretty stable. Today, it is in shambles. The country's gross domestic product fell from $74.76 billions of dollars in 2010 to $29.15 billions in 2015 in part because Libya exported 1.6 million barrels of oil per day in 2010 and only exported 240,000 barrels of oil per day in August 2016.

The inflation is at almost 30 percent. Youth unemployment is at 48 percent and the banking system is on the brink of collapse. In the short term, Libya must manage fiscal spending pressures while restoring and improving basic public services.

In the long term, Libya needs to develop a more diversified market-based economy that goes beyond the oil and gas sector. But in the limited term, Libya should invest in new management of oil and gas revenues to ensure they are using the best interest of the whole country.

The private sector will only be able to reenter the Libya market once the security situation is stabilized. But then it can help create sustainable jobs and wealth.

For the unemployed, targeted intervention should seek advanced skills development, vocational training and apprenticeship and entrepreneurship programs, something that Gaddafi never did but which Libya need in order to have a competitive workforce.

Third, Libya's fractured politics—although there has been some progress in forming national unity government in Libya, unity is today a rather inapplicable word for the country.

Friction between various political actors remain high. One approach to consider is helping Libyans build a confederal state divided into three large regions, for example—Tripolitania, Cyrenaica, and Fezzan.

While a united Libya is preferable, of course, it might be not possible after years of civil war and entrenched hatreds.

So I propose something seemingly paradoxical—deconstructing to construct, which may have the best chance of providing Libyans with a deeper stability. Regional governments could better protect local interests in security, economic reconstruction, and governance.

The international community should have the Libyans start from the bottom, emphasizing local solutions, supporting local actors. The system does not exclude the role of the central government.

[The prepared statement of Ms. Fasanotti follows:]

FEDERICA SAINI FASANOTTI, PhD

Non-Resident Fellow

Center for 21st Century Security and Intelligence

Foreign Policy Program

The Brookings Institution

House Committee on Foreign Affairs

Tuesday, September 27th , 2016

"Libya's Terrorist Devolution: Causes and Solutions"

Libya's persistent fragmentation is what is most worrying today. Internal divisions are the product of decades of Gadhafi's reckless governing: he played his citizens off of each other and kept them isolated from the rest of the world, and also deprived them of any political institution that could keep the country united and stable after he was gone. Libyan history shows that Libyans have long been divided, regionally and locally. Tribes have a long history of fighting one another. Today, the Libyan state remains immature, and those ancient divisions have only gotten worse: at the end of Ghadafi's time, in power there were from 100 to 300 armed militia groups; now there are, according to a European study[1] about 1,600 militias, gangs and criminal groups. UN Security Council Resolution 1970 imposed an arms embargo on Libya, but today there are more than 20 million of weapons circulating in a country of only 6 million people.

External powers who have intervened in Libya have actually worsened the polarization and made reconciliation less likely. It is well know that country such Egypt and Emirates have been supporting the Tobruk government and, on the other side, Qatar and Turkey did the same with the GNC in Tripoli. The state of affairs is still going on, even now that thanks to the UNSMIL mediation in Tripoli has been established a government of National

---

[1] Office of the Commissioner General for Refugees and Stateless Persons (Belgium, Netherlands, Norway and Sweden), *Report: Militias, Tribes and Islamists*, 19 December 2014.

Accord (GNA), presumably recognized by most of international actors. After the 2011 revolution and international intervention, there were few sustainable political options; social frictions increased in the aftermath of Gadhafi's overthrow, and the country's economic fabric corroded. All this only radicalized the insurgency.

The situation in Libya is so compromised that it can be difficult to provide meaningful policy prescriptions. But I must emphasize that Libya's dramatic downward slide is extremely dangerous for the West, and the West should do everything it can to ensure an improvement of the situation. In a territory stretching like Alaska, are active various shades of Islamic terrorism, from the Muslim Brotherhood to al-Qaeda, from Ansal al-Sharia to ISIS. The absence of any state structure has turned the country into the incubator of terrorism, ready to act as a trigger for the whole continent. The nomadic tradition and the experience gained during the Italian domination - handed down from generation to generation - has provided to the Libyans the ability to survive and recover strength even after the heaviest defeats.

In my opinion there are three key challenges we have to address: the security situation, the severe economic downturn, and deeply fractured politics. These factors are all intertwined, and you cannot tackle one if you have not invested in the other.

First, security. Libya is a country at war today. Criminals and their networks are increasingly well-organized. The state police are powerless even when they exist, and the armed forces no longer exist as a coherent entity (in spite of efforts by some Western countries). The problem of criminals and militias is connected to the huge amount of weapons, so the first thing to do is try to diminish them. One policy could be to consider a "weapons buy-back" program, which has actually been implemented in Afghanistan in recent years, even though in Libya the situation presents many social and economic differences. In the medium term, it is essential that the Libyan Armed Forces, National Security Forces and the local police be fundamentally rebuilt.

Second, the economy. Before the revolution, Libya's oil-based economy was functional and pretty stable. Today, it is in shambles. The country's gross domestic product (GDP) fell from $74.76 billion in 2010 to $29.15 billion in 2015, in part because Libya exported 1.6 million barrels of oil per day in 2010 and only exported 240,000 barrels of oil per day in August 2016. Inflation is at almost 30%, youth unemployment is at 48%, and the banking system is on the brink of collapse. In the short term, Libya must manage fiscal spending pressures while restoring and improving basic public services. In the long term, Libya — hopefully with help from the international community—needs to develop a more diversified, market-based economy that goes beyond the oil and gas sector. But in the immediate term, Libya should invest in a new management of oil and gas revenues to ensure they are used in the best interests of the whole country. The private sector will only be able to re-enter the Libyan market once the security situation stabilizes, but then it can help create sustainable jobs and wealth. For the unemployed, targeted interventions should seek advance skills development, vocational training, and apprenticeship and entrepreneurship programs—something that Gadhafi never did, but which Libya needs in order to have a competitive workforce.

Third, Libya's fractured politics. Although there has been some progress in forming a national unity government in Libya, "unity" is today a rather inapplicable word for the country. Friction between various political actors remains high. One approach to consider is helping Libyans build a confederal state, divided into three large regions: Tripolitania, Cyrenaica, and Fezzan. While a united Libya is preferable, it might not be possible after years of civil war and entrenched hatreds. So I propose something seemingly paradoxical: deconstructing to construct, which may have the best chance of providing Libyans with a deeper stability. Regional governments could better protect local interests in security, economic reconstruction, and governance. The international community should thus help the Libyans start from the bottom, emphasizing local solutions, supporting local actors, and helping to empower Libyans to choose their leaders at a local level. The system does not exclude the role of the central government in managing and redistributing resources and conducting other important functions such as foreign policy and borders control.

This would mean that such a government would be less influential in the daily life of Libyans. It's an incredibly difficult and long plan, but probably the only one that can work.

Mr. COOK. Thank you very much.

Our next witness, Mr. Joscelyn.

STATEMENT OF MR. THOMAS JOSCELYN, SENIOR EDITOR, LONG WAR JOURNAL, FOUNDATION FOR DEFENSE OF DE-MOCRACIES

Mr. JOSCELYN. Well, Congressman, thank you for having me here today to testify before you. Last time I testified on Libya specifically was before Homeland Security in April 2011 and I testified then that we should be wary the jihadis will take advantage of the political vacuum and the uprisings and expand their presence.

Little did I know that within just days before I testified actually Osama bin Laden had received a memo in his compound in Abbottabad, Pakistan that specifically outlined how they were going to send operatives who had been freed from custody in Iran and elsewhere to Libya to take advantage of the uprisings and they were going to establish their beachhead in Libya.

So al-Qaeda actually very much saw what was going on in Libya as an opportunity to expand their operations and they did so. I am going to start by talking about the Islamic State, which is sort of the hot brand of the moment but then I am going to come back to al-Qaeda.

As you said, Congressman Zeldin, Libya is crucially important for the Islamic State. Earlier this year in May, Abu Muhammad al Adnani, who was the Islamic State spokesman, was killed in August, actually mentioned Sirte as one of the top three cities on the Islamic State's priority list.

He mentioned it alongside Raqqa and Mosul as sort of key areas under the organization's control. The good news today is that Sirte is on the verge of falling, that basically local Libyan forces backed by American air strikes in our Operation Odyssey Lightning have absolutely dislodged the Islamic State from much of the city and the surrounding areas.

The bad news is we don't really know, or at least I don't know, how many forces the Islamic State has throughout Libya in its entirety. There is others that mentioned there are other areas in the south, in Benghazi and elsewhere, the Islamic State continues to operate.

My suspicion is that they've basically redeployed some of their forces from Sirte, which they are on the verge of losing entirely, to other areas in Libya.

So the key question in Libya is the key question that comes in Iraq and Syria as well—what comes next after they lose their safe haven. We know that the Islamic State is still able to maintain a prolific insurgency, conduct massive terrorist attacks within the country and will be able to sort of continue to facilitate sort of the movement of its operatives.

The Islamic State—something I call ISIS fever has sort of infected our coverage of jihadi groups. There is no about that ISIS has grown substantially and is a big problem. I am not discounting that. But it also obscures in some ways what's going on in the other side of the jihadi coin with al-Qaeda. And I saw a documentary, for example, earlier this year on PBS Frontline, which was excellent in many ways, which focused on ISIS in Benghazi.

13

And if you'd watched this documentary you would have thought that the only jihadi game in Benghazi was the Islamic State when in fact by our count the Islamic State is probably less than 10 percent of jihadi operations in Benghazi currently.

And al-Qaeda has in fact established front groups in Libya through which they are operating to this day. Going back to 2011-2012, remember the rise of Ansar al-Sharia.

Well, the big meme on Ansar al-Sharia is it really isn't al-Qaeda, right. Well, that was all theater. It was all false.

In fact, when the head of Ansar al-Sharia, Muhammad al-Zawahi, was killed, al-Qaeda came out with a statement saying in fact he had met with Osama bin Laden personally in the 1990s and adopted al-Qaeda's methodology then and in fact he was personally eulogized by Ayman al-Zawahiri.

And there are now designations by the U.N. and just voluminous material on the fact that Ansar al-Sharia was, in fact, and is a front group for al-Qaeda and their operations, in particular, al-Qaeda and the Islamic Maghreb.

But what I'd say to that—an additional point of that is there are other organizations in Libya today that are connected to al-Qaeda. What we do in Long War Journal is what I call nerd analysis where we track operatives and what they are saying and propaganda—those sorts of things—to try and detect sort of the hints of al-Qaeda's presence—that they are very keen to hide, I would say.

And as we have this hearing today, keep in mind that the Islamic State declared its presence in Sirte as a new sort of one of its trio of capitals for its operations. Al-Qaeda has not done the same thing in Libya or elsewhere. This is by deliberate design.

Al-Qaeda looks at what the Islamic State is doing and it said well before even the Islamic State's rise and say if you prematurely declare an Islamic State and then you can't hold it you have discredited this idea not only amongst jihadis but also amongst the Muslim population and therefore al-Qaeda is basically looking at the loss of Sirte and is looking at the loss of territory in Syria and Iraq and then saying, we told you so.

This is the message we see because we track in Arabic and other languages on a day to day basis that's going out right now and they are saying it in Libya itself as well.

And so as that warning was expressed by Ayman al-Zawahiri and other al-Qaeda leaders, I have no doubt that they are looking to take advantage of the fact the Islamic State is losing ground in Libya as well.

Now, this doesn't mean that al-Qaeda is this sort of 10-foot ogre in Libya. They are not. But they have taken their lumps as well and they've lost quite a bit of personnel in the war in Libya.

But as we move forward in this hearing I just wanted to keep in mind that just because group doesn't call itself al-Qaeda doesn't mean it isn't al-Qaeda and that al-Qaeda is still very present in Libya to this day.

Thank you.

[The prepared statement of Mr. Joscelyn follows:]

CONGRESSIONAL TESTIMONY: FOUNDATION FOR DEFENSE OF DEMOCRACIES

House Foreign Affairs Committee
Subcommittee on Terrorism, Nonproliferation, and Trade

Libya's Terrorist Descent:
Causes and
Solutions

THOMAS JOSCELYN

Senior Fellow
Foundation for Defense of Democracies

Senior Editor
The Long War Journal

Washington, DC
September 27, 2016

FDD
FOUNDATION FOR
DEFENSE OF DEMOCRACIES

www.defenddemocracy.org

Chairman Poe, Ranking Member Keating and members of the subcommittee, thank you for inviting me here today to discuss the turmoil in Libya. Obviously, the multi-sided conflict in Libya is complex, with various forces pulling the country in multiple directions. My testimony today focuses on the jihadist groups operating inside Libya, especially the Islamic State's arm and groups belonging to al Qaeda's network. I am going to emphasize five key points:

1. The Islamic State is on the verge of losing its safe haven in Sirte, Libya. The loss of Sirte would be a major blow to the so-called caliphate, as Abu Bakr al Baghdadi's organization has invested significant resources in this state-building project. From the Islamic State's perspective, Sirte was one of the most important cities under its control. This was true even though most of the city's citizens had fled the jihadists' occupation. By controlling Sirte, the Islamic State was able to portray its "caliphate" as having significant territory outside of Iraq and Syria. If Baghdadi's loyalists are cleared from Sirte in the coming weeks, then the U.S. and its allies should trumpet the group's loss. During its rise to power, the Islamic State's motto was "remaining and expanding." This was a key part of the organization's marketing message. But in Libya, as in Iraq and Syria, it is no longer true.

2. Despite losing its grip on Sirte and the surrounding towns and villages, however, the Islamic State will retain a presence inside Libya. The group has cadres in Benghazi and elsewhere. The Islamic State's leaders likely evacuated some of their men from Sirte as the offensive on the city progressed. It is important to note that even though the Islamic State is on the verge of a significant defeat, the effort required a robust commitment by local Libyan ground forces, as well as more than 170 "precision" American airstrikes to date. As the Islamic State's men have been cleared block by block from Sirte, they have demonstrated that they continue maintain a strong operational capacity, launching suicide bombings in neighborhoods they've lost and killing dozens of their Libyan enemies. The U.S. and its partners will have to make sure that they hold Sirte once it is cleared, as well as prevent the Islamic State from seizing significant terrain elsewhere.

3. The Islamic State's loss of Sirte will be viewed in jihadist circles as a vindication of al Qaeda's strategy. Al Qaeda's senior leaders, including Osama bin Laden and Ayman al Zawahiri, repeatedly warned that the premature declaration of an Islamic state harms the jihadists' cause. Al Qaeda in the Islamic Maghreb's (AQIM) emir, Abdulmalek Droukdel, has made the same argument. Al Qaeda has consistently argued that a jihadist state cannot survive if the U.S. and its allies decide to intervene. This is exactly what happened in Sirte.

4. Some assume that, unlike the Islamic State, al Qaeda does not seek to control territory and build Islamic emirates (states). But this is an erroneous assumption. A wealth of evidence shows that this is, in fact, al Qaeda's primary goal. However, al Qaeda and the Islamic State have very different strategies for achieving this same end. AQIM and its allies briefly controlled much of Mali beginning in 2012. Documents recovered in Mali show that AQIM was laying the groundwork for an Islamic state. But Droukdel and his advisors concluded that their effort needed to be firmly rooted in the host society, so AQIM was willing to partner with tribes and organizations that did not share its ideology. AQIM is following a version of this same strategy inside Libya today and has been working to embed itself in various local groups and communities. The Islamic State's model for state-building is top-down authoritarian. In the view of Baghdadi and his key advisors, all Muslims must submit to the so-called caliphate's authority. Al Qaeda's follows a bottom-up plan, which means that the organization is seeking to spread the jihadist ideology, win popular support and embed itself within local societies. Al Qaeda and AQIM, which is openly loyal to Ayman al Zawahiri, are not close to achieving their goals in many areas. But the al Qaeda network remains deeper than many assume.

5. In addition to the assistance the U.S. military provides local forces, the U.S. government should work to expose al Qaeda's network inside Libya. Sun light is a key part of any plan to combat al Qaeda's clandestine strategy. Al Qaeda's senior leadership has dispatched operatives to Libya in the past. AQIM doesn't typically advertise its presence in Libya, but has clearly backed groups such as Ansar al Sharia in Libya and the

Mujahideen Shura Council in Derna. Indeed, al Qaeda has worked under multiple brand names in Libya.

The importance of Sirte to the Islamic State

In May, the Islamic State's spokesman, Abu Muhammad al Adnani, revealed just how important Sirte is to the caliphate-building project. Adnani, who was subsequently killed in an airstrike in August, mentioned Sirte alongside Raqqa, Syria and Mosul, Iraq in a speech entitled, "That They Live By Proof." Raqqa and Mosul are the de facto capitals of the group's self-declared caliphate. By rhetorically elevating Sirte to the same status as these two cities, Adnani signaled just how significant the North African locale really was for the Islamic State's long-term plans.

Indeed, the Islamic State dispatched key figures to Libya to build a beachhead for the organization. In November 2015, for instance, the U.S. military conducted its first airstrike against an Islamic State leader in Libya. According to the Department of Defense, the bombing targeted Abu Nabil, also known as Wissam Najm Abd Zayd al Zubaydi, "an Iraqi national who was a longtime al Qaeda operative and the senior ISIL leader in Libya."[1] Nabil "may have been the spokesman in the February 2015 Coptic Christian execution video," DOD noted, referring to a mass execution on Libya's shores that the Islamic State celebrated in one of its typically grotesque propaganda productions. Nabil was hardly the only senior Islamic State leader sent to Libya. The organization sent trained cadres of fighters from North Africa to Libya to help with its expansion plans, and also worked to recruit defectors from existing jihadist organizations, such as Ansar al Sharia.[2]

The same month that Adnani delivered his speech on Mosul, Raqqa and Sirte (May 2015), Al Bunyan Al Marsoos ("Solid Structure") operations room began its offensive on the Islamic

---

[1] See: http://www.defense.gov/News/News-Releases/News-Release-View/Article/628954/statement-from-pentagon-press-secretary-peter-cook-on-us-strike-in-libya

[2] However, Ansar al Shara as a whole did not defect to the Islamic State, but instead remained loyal to al Qaeda.

State's Libyan stronghold. Al Bunyan Al Marsoos draws fighters from militias based in Misrata and is allied with Libya's Government of National Accord (GNA). The assault quickly gained ground, but stalled by July. On August 1, the U.S. began to launch airstrikes in support of the operations room. As of September 25, according to U.S. Africa Command, there have been a total of 175 airstrikes as part of Operation Odyssey Lightning.[3]

During testimony before the Senate Armed Services Committee on September 22, Secretary of Defense Ash Carter explained that he and other U.S. officials had "expressed concern that if left untended, Libya could be the next ISIL [Islamic State] headquarters, as ISIL's control over the city of Sirte was seen as their contingency plan for where they would go when they lost Raqqa and Mosul."[4] However, because of the American airstrikes and the heavy load carried by local fighters, the Islamic State's safe haven had been "reduced to a single square kilometer" in "a single neighborhood," Carter said. A map produced by Al Bunyan Al Marsoos echoed this assessment.[5]

Therefore, the Islamic State appears to be on the verge of a key loss. However, we should be mindful that the Islamic State's manpower has been drastically underestimated in the past. Given that much of Libya's south is remote and ungoverned, the Islamic State could find areas to regroup. Also, Baghdadi's men are fighting in Benghazi and elsewhere. In my view, their presence in Benghazi has been exaggerated, to a degree, but they clearly have cadres fighting on the ground inside the city today. The Islamic State may have also redeployed some of its forces to Benghazi and Derna as a result of the situation in Sirte. Earlier this year, the group was forced out of Derna by jihadists connected to al Qaeda's network. But it is possible that some fighters will return to Derna, or the city's outskirts, now that they no longer have a safe haven in Sirte.

Al Qaeda's long-term approach to state-building

---

[3] See: http://www.africom.mil/NewsByCategory/pressrelease/28413/u-s-airstrikes-in-support-of-gna-sept-23-to-25

[4] See: http://www.armed-services.senate.gov/imo/media/doc/Carter_09-22-16.pdf

[5] The map can be viewed here: http://www.longwarjournal.org/archives/2016/09/islamic-states-safe-haven-in-sirte-libya-shrinks-to-a-single-neighborhood.php

Unlike the Islamic State, which advertises and even exaggerates its presence in some areas, al Qaeda is keen to avoid scrutiny. Al Qaeda has developed an entirely different strategy for operating in countries such as Libya. Al Qaeda sees jihadi state-building as a long-term endeavor that requires strategic patience. The Islamic State deliberately played off of this strategy to quickly grow in size, capitalizing on younger jihadis' and new recruits' impatience. In essence, the Islamic State marketed itself by asking a simple question: Why wait for al Qaeda's caliphate to come in the future, or maybe never, when you can come fight for the "caliphate" today?

The Islamic State's approach allowed it to mushroom in the short-term, but its long-term liabilities are now being exposed in Iraq, Syria and Libya. Al Qaeda knew all along that the Islamic State's caliphate claim would prove to be tenuous, and al Qaeda's strategy will now be vindicated in some jihadis' eyes. In this section, I am going to reference three key documents to illuminate al Qaeda's strategy. All three of them were produced by either AQIM or another part of al Qaeda.

An especially important document for understanding al Qaeda's thinking is a letter written by AQIM's emir, Abdulmalek Droukdel, to the shura council of Ansar Dine, which AQIM used as its local face.[6] Although Droukdel's missive was written with Mali in mind, the lessons he outlined are equally applicable to Libya. Droukdel argued that "the great powers with hegemony over the international situation, despite their weakness and their retreat caused by military exhaustion and the financial crisis, still have many cards to play that enable them to prevent the creation of an Islamic state in Azawad ruled by the jihadis and Islamists."

That is, in Droukdel's view, Western powers could easily overrun a jihadi state ruled by al Qaeda and its partners. Even though AQIM and its allies seized much of Mali in 2012, Droukdel urged caution. "We must not go too far or take risks in our decisions or imagine that this project is a stable Islamic state," Droukdel wrote. Instead, the jihadis should view it as an "important golden

---

[6] The document was first reported on by Rukmini Callimachi, then with the Associated Press and now with *The New York Times*. The memo can be found online here:
http://hosted.ap.org/specials/interactives/_international/_pdfs/al-qaida-manifesto.pdf

opportunity to extend bridges to the various sectors and parts of Azawad society" in northern Mali, including Arabs, the Tuareg people, and other Africans. This would "end the situation of political and social and intellectual separation (or isolation) between the Mujahideen and these sectors, particularly the big tribes, and the main rebel movements with their various ideologies, and the elite of Azawad society, its clerics, its groupings, its individuals and its noble forces." Simply put, Droukdel was concerned with building broader popular support for the jihadists' agenda.

Droukdel wanted to make sure that the jihadists' attempt at governance had a local face, such that AQIM did not "monopolize the political and military stage" and was not "at the forefront." AQIM's chief argued that they should work closely with other parties, such as the Azawad Liberation Movement, to administer the new state. Sharia law should be implemented only gradually, in Droukdel's opinion, as the population was not accustomed to living under al Qaeda's Draconian penal code. (Al Qaeda's branches have adopted this same approach in Syria and Yemen.)

Should the emirate fall, which Droukdel thought was "very probable," then the jihadists would not bear the responsibility by themselves and would have at least planted a "good seed in this fertile soil…so that the tree will grow more quickly" in the future. "We look forward to seeing this tree as it will be: stable and magnificent," Droukdel wrote. The AQIM chief mixed metaphors by also comparing the jihadist project in Mali to a "small newborn" who is "crawling on [his] knees, and has not yet stood on [his] two legs."

Droukdel concluded that AQIM had "two missions" and combining them created a "true dilemma." AQIM wanted to both preserve the "Azawad Islamic project," meaning the effort to build an Islamist state, and also continue its "global jihadi project." The latter is a reference to AQIM's commitment to carrying out terrorist operations throughout the region. Droukdel and his advisors came up with two proposals. In the first scenario, AQIM would subordinate itself to the local ruler. AQIM would "be under the emirate of Ansar Dine" such that AQIM's "emir would follow their emir" and AQIM's "opinion would follow their opinion." This would be the case for all "internal activity," meaning "all activity connected to participating in bearing the responsibilities of the liberated areas." But all "external activity" connected to the "global jihad...would be independent of them (Ansar Dine)" and AQIM "would ensure that none of that activity or its repercussions is attributed to them [Ansar Dine], as care must be taken over negative impacts on the project of the state."[7]

In Droukdel's "second proposal," some of al Qaeda's mujahideen "would be set aside and put under the complete control of the emir of Ansar Dine to participate in bearing the burden of running the affairs of the liberated cities." The remaining al Qaeda members would be "completely independent of Ansar Dine and its activity would be limited to jihadi action outside the region."[8]

AQIM never got the chance to fully implement either of one of the strategies Droukdel outlined in his memo. Just as Droukdel feared, the jihadists' nascent state in Mali was quickly dismantled after France intervened in early 2013. But Droukdel's memo illustrates just how different al Qaeda's thinking is from the Islamic State's. Whereas Abu Bakr al Baghdadi's men have advertised their presence in the form of "provinces" of the so-called caliphate, al Qaeda's loyalists have decided that it is foolish to declare Islamic emirates, or states, anywhere. In fact, Al Qaeda's leaders often do not want outside observers to know that their organization is present at all.

There is ample evidence demonstrating that AQIM has followed this same strategy in Libya. In March, al Qaeda released the seventh issue of its Al Masra newsletter. The Arabic publication included an article featuring a senior AQIM leader known as Abu Abdul Ilah Ahmed. Ahmed discussed AQIM's game plan for Libya at length, saying the group had the opportunity to establish an Islamic state in Libya, but decided such a move would be premature. Instead, Ahmed said, AQIM decided to back groups such Ansar al Sharia, the Abu Salim Martyrs

---

[7] It should be noted that Droukdel's words invite a comparison to the current situation in Syria, where al Qaeda's leadership did not want anti-Western plotting to spoil the jihadis' role in the war against Bashar al Assad's regime. In Syria, as elsewhere, al Qaeda embedded itself deeply within the fabric of the insurgency, making it difficult, if not impossible, to separate the jihadis from more acceptable rebel groups.

[8] Again, one can easily draw a comparison to the situation in Syria, where Al Nusrah Front has been rebranded as Jabhat Fath al Sham and distanced itself from anti-Western terrorism in an attempt to maintain a clean brand for the fight against Assad.

Brigade (ASMB) in Derna, and the faithful shura councils that were established in several Libyan cities. Ahmed stressed that Ansar al Sharia and ASMB have the same goals as AQIM, as they are all fighting to establish sharia in Libya.[9] AQIM's man added that it is the "duty" of all mujahideen to "unite," but such an effort requires "time" and "sacrifices from all parties."

An especially telling passage in Ahmed's discussion focused on whether or not AQIM has an official arm in Libya. Ahmed portrayed AQIM as being one with the Libyan people in the fight against "America and its Crusader alliance," adding that AQIM will back the Libyan people against the French, who are "violating the sanctity of Libya." AQIM is not focused on collecting pledges of allegiance at this juncture, Ahmed pointed out, but is instead rallying the people against foreign "aggression." Ahmed framed AQIM's war as part of a long jihadi tradition dating back to Omar al Mukhtar, who resisted Italian forces in Libya in the early part of the 20th Century. This is a consistent AQIM theme, as the group has portrayed its men as the "progeny of Omar al Mukhtar."[10]

Another key document is an analysis by a prolific jihadi writer known as Abdullah bin Mohammed, who has been identified as an al Qaeda member and strategist.[11] Bin Mohammed has a large audience on social media, with more than 350,000 accounts following him (@strateeegy) on Twitter. In early 2015, bin Mohammed published an article entitled, "Political Guerrilla Warfare," in which he argued that jihadists needed to be more flexible in their dealings with other Islamist parties.

Bin Mohammed likened his ideas to the military strategy Osama bin Laden and al Qaeda's other leaders devised for confronting the West. Bin Mohammed explained that Bin Laden realized al Qaeda could not defeat the U.S. and its allies in a straight fight, so al Qaeda relied on high-profile terrorist attacks and guerrilla warfare to confront its superior foes. "The military

---

9 The ASMB is one of the major players in the Mujahideen Shura Council in Derna.
10 See Thomas Joscelyn, "Al Qaeda in the Islamic Maghreb squadron ambushed in Libya," *The Long War Journal*, November 30, 2015. Available at: http://www.longwarjournal.org/archives/2015/11/aqim-squadron-ambushed-in-libya.php

11 Ali Hashem, "Al-Qaeda theorist calls for infiltrating political systems," *Al Monitor*, May 29, 2015. (Available at: http://www.al-monitor.com/pulse/originals/2015/05/al-qaeda-political-system-infiltration.html)

23

calculations proved to us that an open confrontation with a strong enemy like the U.S. is military suicide," Bin Mohammed explained in an interview.[12] "Therefore we had to go a different way in military confrontation, and in politics an open confrontation like declaring a state is also political suicide, as the West has the power to weaken us, pressure our societies and at the end uproot us as they did in Afghanistan and Iraq." [13] For these reasons, bin Mohammed explained, "we have to build a new strategy that can enhance our resilience." [14] Bin Mohammed emphasized bin Laden's warning that prematurely declaring an Islamic state is tantamount to "political suicide," as the jihadis' enemies can easily overwhelm them.

Bin Mohammed pointed to the example of the Libyan Islamic Fighting Group (LIFG), whose members have forged alliances with Islamist political parties in Libya. This made it difficult, if not impossible, for the West to thwart the former LIFG members' political designs and also inoculated them from Western counterterrorism pressure. One summary of Bin Mohammed's thesis noted that the LIFG's men have built "solid alliances with other Islamic and revolutionary groups" and are "flexible toward the outside world."[15] Bin Mohammed claimed the LIFG had gone so far as to issue a "fatwa" allowing them "to participate in the democratic regime after they demanded that Sharia be a main source of legislation." In the next step, "they will start working on building their Islamic regime." [16]

Some aspects of Bin Mohammed's thesis proved to be especially controversial within al Qaeda circles. While some saw the wisdom in the strategy Bin Mohammed advocated, others (such as the pro-al Qaeda cleric Abu Qatada) think he went too far. Regardless, al Qaeda is following a version of Bin Mohammed's plan in Libya, Syria and elsewhere. For instance, writing in *Al Monitor* in May 2015, Ali Hashem noted:

It is believed that Mohammed's strategy of political guerrilla war has made its way to being adopted by some of al-Qaeda's affiliated groups, primarily in Syria. Reports have

---

[12] Ibid.
[13] Ibid.
[14] Ibid.
[15] Ibid.
[16] Ibid.

suggested that the Syrian branch of al-Qaeda, Jabhat al-Nusra, might be moving toward a rebranding phase as a result of pressure exerted by allies in the region that want to legitimize the group so it can play a role in Syria's future. The idea to create the Army of Conquest (Jaish al-Fatah), with all the Islamist groups fighting under one banner legitimized by regional and international backers, might well have been influenced by Mohammed's theory.[17]

This is exactly what happened more than one year later. As we reported at *The Long War Journal*, Al Nusrah Front co-founded the Jaysh al Fath (Jaish al-Fatah) alliance as a way to pool the resources of various rebel groups and to prevent al Qaeda's paramilitary army in Syria from being isolated from other factions. Then, in late July 2016, Nusra was rebranded as Jabhat Fath al Sham ("Conquest of the Levant Front") in an attempt to further embed al Qaeda within the Syrian insurgency and to stymie American counterterrorism efforts.

There are direct parallels to the situation in Libya, where al Qaeda has long sought to hide its hand.

Al Qaeda's clandestine presence in Libya

I have outlined al Qaeda's clandestine network in previous testimony and articles, drawing on U.S. and UN terrorism designations, an analysis authored by a Defense Department shop in 2012, primary source evidence produced by the jihadists themselves, as well as other evidence.[18]

---

[17] Ibid.

[18] See, for example, the following: (1) "Global al Qaeda: Affiliates, objectives, and future challenges," Testimony before the House Committee on Foreign Affairs Subcommittee on Terrorism, Nonproliferation, and Trade, July 18, 2013. (Available at:
http://docs.house.gov/meetings/FA/FA18/20130718/101155/HHRG-113-FA18-Wstate-JoscelynT-20130718.pdf); (2) "Terrorism in Africa: The Imminent Threat to the United States," Testimony before the House Committee on Homeland Security's Subcommittee on Counterterrorism and Intelligence, April 29, 2015. (Available at: http://docs.house.gov/meetings/HM/HM05/20150429/103382/HHRG-114-HM05-Wstate-JoscelynT-20150429.pdf); (3) "Al Qaeda's plan for Libya highlighted in congressional report," *The Long War Journal*, September 21, 2012. (Available at:
http://www.longwarjournal.org/archives/2012/09/al_qaedas_plan_for_l.php)

I will not repeat all of that analysis here, but a brief update is necessary because the situation has evolved since I last testified. Three key facts are worth highlighting.

First, the al Qaeda-aligned groups have also sustained serious losses, especially in Benghazi. There, Ansar al Sharia and the Benghazi Revolutionaries Shura Council (BRSC), both of which are part of the al Qaeda network, had led the jihadists in fighting against General Khalifa al Haftar's forces.[19] But this past summer, the jihadists reorganized themselves under the banner of the Benghazi Defense Brigades (BDB). Both Ansar al Sharia and the BRSC are clearly allied with, or part of, the BDB.[20] This is yet another indication that al Qaeda-affiliated jihadists are using front groups and pooling their resources with other organizations inside Libya.

Second, Al Qaeda and affiliated jihadi groups in Libya are rallying around Sheikh Sadiq Al Gharyani, a senior religious figure who is sometimes described as "Libya's Mufti." In July, a statement attributed to Mokhtar Belmokhtar was released online.[21] Belmokhtar heaped praise on Gharyani, saying he "practices what he preaches by exposing the truth in the face of falsehood and its adherents." Belmokhtar asked Allah to "strengthen" Gharyani and his followers such that they are a "fortress for sharia." The Mujahideen Shura Council in Derna (MSCD), which has its own al Qaeda links,[22] views Gharyani has its spiritual figurehead. For instance, the MSCD co-signed a new charter for governing Derna in mid-August. The "charter," which was released on the MSCD's social media sites, referred to Gharyani as the "sole authoritative religious reference." The BDB itself is openly aligned with Gharyani. These moves should be view with suspicion, as it appears AQIM and its Libyan branches are endorsing a "local" face as the rightful governing authority, just as Droukdel advocated in the letter mentioned above.

---

[19] A series of articles demonstrating Ansar al Sharia's ties to the al Qaeda network can be found here: http://www.longwarjournal.org/tags/ansar al sharia-libya.

[20] See: Thomas Joscelyn, "Presence of French special forces in Libya sets off controversy," *The Long War Journal*, July 22, 2016. (Available at: http://www.longwarjournal.org/archives/2016/07/presence-of-french-special-forces-in-libya-sets-off-controversy.php)

[21] Belmokhtar has been reportedly killed on multiple occasions, but his demise was never confirmed. The jihadists, including AQIM, are acting as if he is alive and survived an American airstrike in Libya last year. Thus far, AQIM has not released a proof of life audio or video from Belmokhtar, only written statements. Belmokhtar's Al Murabitoon reunited with AQIM last year. The move was praised by multiple al Qaeda figures.

[22] See: http://www.longwarjournal.org/tags/mujahideen-shura-council-in-derna

Third, AQIM and affiliated groups are seeking to rally support against Western intervention in Libya. For example, Gharyani, AQIM, the BDB and others have strongly denounced France's presence in Benghazi and elsewhere in Libya. Special forces from at least four Western nations (US, UK, France, an Italy) are reportedly operating inside Libya currently. This makes it all the more important for the U.S. and its allies to expose al Qaeda's network inside the country.

———

Mr. COOK. Thank you very much.

Mr. Fishman.

STATEMENT OF MR. BENJAMIN FISHMAN (FORMER DIRECTOR FOR NORTH AFRICA, NATIONAL SECURITY COUNCIL)

Mr. FISHMAN. Thank you for inviting me to appear before you this afternoon. I appreciate this committee's attention to Libya because I believe it remains an important issue for U.S. policy and often it is poorly understood.

My written testimony goes into further details about this but I'd like to highlight just one common misrepresentation. That is if we had left well enough alone, Gaddafi would have returned to his reformed, albeit peculiar, personality.

For those on this committee on terrorism who have not been, I urge you to visit the Pan Am 103 Memorial Cairn at Arlington National Cemetery or participate in the annual memorial there on December 21.

Among other moving tributes, you will see students at Syracuse University—current students—reading out the names of the victims including 35 Syracuse students who were returning home for Christmas.

When I imagine Gaddafi left in power after facing down an uprising in Benghazi, together with his refusal to negotiate anything, I see the man capable of ordering the Pan Am 103 attack, not some humbled strawman—strongman.

Instead of the fragile state that Libya has become, Libya most likely would resemble Syria today and most sides of the conflict could be strongly anti-Western.

I acknowledge that the U.S. and our allies made some errors in handling the post-conflict environment in Libya. There should have been greater involvement with our Libyan partners from day one to help them establish a basic form of governance and security after the 2011 revolution.

But the truth is Libya's leaders didn't want or know how to accept international assistance despite our efforts to help before the security breakdown started emerging and the civil war broke out on 2014 when delivering assistance became less viable.

Now we face a situation where Libya is divided among many factions. The good news is that a unity government, the Government of National Accord, has been formed and there are ongoing efforts to help strengthen that government's legitimacy and credibility.

There is also a dialogue in place to solidify agreement for the unity government, and as my old boss, Ambassador Dennis Ross, says about the Middle East, when the parties are talking directly it strongly reduces the probability of violence.

The process won't be easy but at least it's underway and the GNA has strong international backing from the West and the region.

ISIS and terrorism emanating from Libya remains a current serious concern—the primary reason for holding this hearing. But here, there is actually good news to report.

After ISIS built a so-called government—governate in Libya in the city of Sirte, establishing their Islamic police and executing clerics and other dissidents, local Libyan forces began an offensive against Sirte this summer.

With the support of U.S. air power, Sirte has been virtually liberated from ISIS and we have proven repeatedly through air strikes and capture operations in Libya that the U.S. is capable of doing—capable and interested in sustaining these sorts operations.

The militias from Misrata suffered heavy casualties but they took on the mission themselves. Now, instead of ISIS directing its fighters to Libya, there's no such governate to fall back to in North Africa.

This is not to say that the threat has been vanquished. Terrorism from Libya will evolve and cells will likely be established in Libya's southern desert or, more worrisome, the foreign fighters who made up the bulk of the Sirte contingent may repatriate, posing an especially serious threat to Tunisia. That is why we need to continue to expand our support to the region's only democracy to emerge from the Arab Spring.

In sum, Libya faces many serious challenges. But I must emphasize it is not Syria. It hasn't seen nearly the scale of the violence in Aleppo alone. Nor is it Yemen. Both countries pose far greater threats to regional security and to U.S. interests in the homeland and overseas.

I still believe Libya has a chance to realize the vision of the 2011 revolution and we should do whatever we can together with our allies to assist the Libyans to achieve this goal.

Thank you, and I look forward to your questions.

[The prepared statement of Mr. Fishman follows:]

Benjamin Fishman
Former Director for North Africa at the National Security Council
Editor of *North Africa in Transition: The Struggle for Democracies and Institutions*

House Committee on Foreign Affairs
Subcommittee on Terrorism, Nonproliferation, and Trade
Hearing on Libya's Terrorist Devolution: Causes and Solutions
Tuesday October 27, 2016

Chairman Poe, Ranking Member Keating:

Thank you for inviting me to appear before you this afternoon.

I have been closely following events in Libya and U.S. policy since March 2011, shortly after the Libyan revolution against Qaddafi erupted and President Obama decided to support a UN-authorized, NATO-led coalition to protect the people of Libya from an impending massacre in Benghazi. I served on the National Security Council at the time and worked to coordinate our government's participation in NATO's Operation Unified Protector and our subsequent efforts to work with the UN and our allies to support post-conflict reconstruction and a democratic transition. I left the government in the fall of 2013 and have been following and writing about Libya since.

This hearing is intended to focus on possible solutions to Libya's current challenges, specifically regarding its threat as a breading ground and safe haven for terrorism. Before addressing these important issues, I'd first like to dispel some common misrepresentations about how Libya's transition went off course.

Misrepresentation 1: We should never have gone into Libya in the first place; the threat was not significant to the U.S. or the Libyan population; Qaddafi could have been placated.

There was a legitimate debate about whether the U.S. should get involved in a domestic conflict in Libya. Secretary of Defense Robert Gates was the leading voice of dissent in the cabinet at the time, along with Vice President Biden. Secretary Gates argued that Libya held little direct interest for U.S. policy in the region and did not want to divert import assets and resources from the ongoing conflicts in Iraq and Afghanistan.

Ultimately, the president designed an operation to blunt Qaddafi's attack, protect Libya's population, dedicating our "unique capabilities" such as aerial refueling and intelligence, surveillance, and reconnaissance assets while insisting that our NATO and regional partners step up and implement the UNSCR by conducting the appropriate airstrikes. President Obama was clear from the beginning that U.S.

participation would involve no U.S. boots on the ground, would require regional and international support (manifested by UNSCR 1973 and the Arab League's endorsement), and limit our contributions to the unique capabilities previously referenced. Six months later, with the support of the NATO coalition, Qaddafi met his fate and Libya became free of his 42-year brutal dictatorial rule.

Several critics from Russian leaders to academic skeptics have argued that UNSCR 1973 was never supposed to authorize regime change in Libya, especially after the immediate threat against Benghazi was stopped by the initial bombings in March 2011. Other critics argue that we should never gotten involved in Libya and that Qaddafi should have been left in power. After all, he had given up his nuclear weapons program after the 2003 invasion of Iraq and had agreed to the destruction of his chemical weapons. He became a partner against al-Qaeda (which was also opposed to his rule. And he had allowed the beginning of domestic reforms spearheaded by his son Saif al-Islam.

Although no counterfactual can be proven, this rosy vision of a post-revolution Qaddafi is a fantasy. Challenged by his people, he would have undoubtedly carried out his threats to hunt every dissident out "like rats." He was irreconcilable and didn't even receive a UN-appointed envoy to discuss possible terms for a negotiated transition. A host of friendly envoys from South African president Jacob Zuma, to an African Union Delegation, to a Russian chess champion made no impression. Lower level outreach only elicited similar intransigence. I have no doubt that were he left in power without a clear path to a negotiated transition, Qaddafi, a terrorist responsible for the deaths of Americans on Pan-AM 103 and other brutal attacks at home and abroad, would have returned to his terrorist ways.

For those on this committee on terrorist who have not been, I urge you to visit the Pan-AM memorial cairn at Arlington National Cemetery or participate in the annual memorial there on December 21. Among other moving tributes, you will see students at Syracuse University reading out the names of the victims, including the 35 Syracuse students who were returning home for Christmas. When I imagine a Qaddafi left in power after facing down an uprising in Benghazi together with his refusal to negotiate anything, his threats to his own population and his history as an international terrorist, I see the man capable of ordering the Pan-Am 103 attack, not some humbled benign strongman. Instead of the fragile state that Libya has become (and discussed below) Libya most likely would resemble Syria – and both sides of the conflict could be virulently anti-Western.

Misrepresentation 2: NATO and the U.S. abandoned Libya after the intervention; there should have been a stabilization force assembled to restore security.

The other common misrepresentations about post-conflict Libya is that with better planning or some kind on stabilization force similar to the deployments in the Balkans or East Timor, Libya could have been stabilized and a terrorism problem would have never have emerged. Unfortunately, such a prospect was never in the cards. No country from NATO or outside was eager to lead such a theoretical peacekeeping operation, and the Libyans rejected the prospect of such a visible international presence. The Libyans wanted to own their future and were always wary of accepting too much help from the outside. They were willing to accept the concept of training and technical assistance on a range of issues, which were offered by us and our allies coordinated by the UN. But when it came to pinning down the details, it proved an endlessly circuitous path.

There were some initially positive signs. Libyans enthusiastically voted in their first free and fair democratic election in 2012. Oil production was quickly restored to its prewar level (which ironically discouraged foreign governments to pay for international assistance in Libya, a nominally wealthy country), and civil society and free media started to blossom.

Unfortunately, and tragically for Libya, security events started to emerge coinciding with deepening political rifts between so called secular-moderate parties and Islamist-revolution factions. This is not the forum to rehash Benghazi, but I cannot underscore enough how much the tragedy effectively limited our ability to influence events on the ground going forward. We lost our Ambassador, a close colleague and friend, along with three other brave Americans. Our Embassy in Tripoli was not only leaderless and demoralized but its ability to carry out its normal work of reporting and programming was virtually halted as a result of security considerations. The attack further widened the divisions between Libya's factions and weakened the interim government.

After another contested election whose legitimacy was challenged by one party, Libya effective split into two governments, the House of Representatives (HoR) in the east, and the General National Congress (GNC) in Tripoli. A civil war ensued and the violence forced out international embassies in the summer of 2014. Throughout 2015, the UN worked actively with a National Dialogue Committee and both parties to develop the Libya Political Agreement (LPA), a complicated arrangement that would create a Presidency Council (PC) and incorporate the HoR as a legislative body and involve the GNC as an advisory council. The nine-person PC was formed in March 2016 headed by Prime Minister Fayez al-Serraj. As of this hearing, the HoR is still disputing the terms of the LPA and has rejected Serraj's proposed cabinet

Libya's political fragility contributes to its security challenges. The PC needs to establish greater legitimacy in part by addressing key issues of governance: electricity, fuel and medical supply shortages are too common; a liquidity crisis has incentivized the black market for local currency. The UN has established a development fund to assist with critical short-term infrastructure needs but it will be hard to implement projects (challenging in Libya in any circumstances given its unreformed bureaucracy) due to security concerns.

The Terrorism Threat Today

Libya has always featured an aggressive jihadist element dating back at least to the 1980's where a contingent of Libyans was influential in Afghanistan. Upon their return, they formed the Libyan Islamic Fighting Group and fought an insurgency against Qaddafi in the east. Through a combination of military losses and imprisonments, the LIFG entered into negotiations with the regime and agreed to disband and reform in exchange for releasing many of its prisoners, including some shortly before the 2011 revolution.

Although the LIFG no longer exists, many of its former members assumed prominent roles in the revolution and post-revolutionary government. There is a complicated and still unclear relationship between these former jihadists, al-Qaeda, and Libya's governing institutions. Some, like General Khalifa Heftar, the eastern general and a party to Libya's civil war, as well as his backers in Egypt and the UAE, believe that all Islamists, from the Muslim Brotherhood's political party, to former LIFG member and former parliamentarian Abdel-Hakim Belhajj, to ISIS, are just different shades of the same enemy. Others recognize that there is and will always be some Islamist presence in Libya and the key to stability is to find a compromise that includes the moderates among them in the political process rather than to encourage their irreconcilable opposition. That debate could determine Libya's future stability.

In the midst of Libya's civil war, ISIS managed to set up a province in Sirte in early 2015 (after being repulsed by local jihadists in Derna). ISIS clearly took advantage of Libya's instability to install itself and adopt its brutal form of Islamic rule. Initial attempts by local militias to oust ISIS from Sirte were repulsed. As a result, it had over a year to entrench itself in the city, during which ISIS leaders from Syria encouraged foreign fighters to go to Libya given the prospect of territorial loss in Iraq and Syria. Initial intelligence estimates suggested that ISIS had 5000-7000 fighters in Sirte but reports from Libyans suggest the figure was much lower. Importantly, many of these fighters were from outside Libya, including from Tunisia, Sudan and elsewhere in the region. That proved advantageous for organizing an offensive against ISIS because Libyans reject the concept of foreign occupation, whether from a western democracy or a jihadist group. Moreover, most Libyans are conservative Muslims, and many follow the Sufi traditions; to them, ISIS' distortions of Islam are anathema.

In July, a militia coalition from Misrata loyal to the Government of National Accord (GNA) pushed back ISIS, which had expanded along the coastline, to Sirte's city limits where they suffered heavy casualties in the urban environment from IEDs and snipers. At the request of the PC, the U.S. began targeted airstrikes against ISIS in Sirte on August 1st using unmanned drones, attack helicopters, and Harrier jets. To date, AFRICOM has conducted over 100 strikes against heavy weaponry and fighting positions, enabling the militias to liberate most of the city. Although ISIS's safe haven in Libya has been mostly eliminated, there is still the risk that the group could regroup in cells throughout Libya's poorly governed territories and its foreign fighters could repatriate, posing a critical threat especially to Tunisia.

Beyond the Sirte operation, the U.S. has proven willing and able to conduct targeted CT operations in Libya against ISIL and other jihadist targets. In 2013, U.S. Special Forces captured Abu Anas Al-Libi in Tripoli, the perpetrator of the 1998 East Africa embassy bombings. In June 2014, the U.S. captured Ahmed Abu Kattalah who is charged with leading the attack on the U.S. Special Mission in Benghazi. Khattalah is in custody a few miles away. The U.S. has also carried targeted airstrikes against suspected terrorist cells, including one against a suspected AQIM leader near the eastern city of Ajdabiya and one against the ISIS training cell in Sebratha thought to be responsible for the attacks against the Bardo museum in Tunis and the beach resort in Sirte that have devastated Tunisia's tourist industry.

In other words, U.S. counterterrorism policy in Libya has been effective. It has blunted ISIS' effort to establish a safe haven in Libya and taken many fighters off the battlefield. And it has targeted key personalities and cells and remains vigillent to additional opportunities. The challenge will be continuing to align these CT efforts with a slow political process that is necessary to stabilize the country.

Looking Ahead

The most effective way that the U.S. and our allies can continue to alleviate the terror threat posed from Libya is to continue working aggressively to help settle the country's ongoing disputes over political unity. An effective CT policy requires a credible and effective local partner. Therefore, as a first priority, we must support the Government of National Accord, help it to govern by providing technical assistance and development funds, such as the recently announced UN Stabilization Fund. Together with our allies, we must also do whatever possible to ensure that the GNA alone receives the profits from oil exports, and that, in turn, its oil facilities are protected by neutral forces to exports and grow exports. Finally, we must continue to pressure the supporters of those blocking the unity process, primarily Egypt, to halt their counterproductive behavior.

In terms of directly countering ISIS, we must build up intelligence resources in the region, support Tunisia with greater security – and economic assistance given their mutually reinforcing relationship – and help our international partners build up a neutral, professional security force that can protect state institutions and form the backbone of a counterterror force.

Mr. Cook. Thank you very much.

My first question I want to ask is—and I know that you're all experts on Libya but I want to get your feelings about Egypt because, obviously, Egypt has had problems in the Sinai.

They've had a history in the past going back quite a few years now where they almost went to war or were at war with Libya in the past.

But Islamic extremists in Libya would that cause a military or at least a diplomatic reaction from el-Sisi, in your opinion? Anybody? Doctor?

Ms. Fasanotti. Yes. I think that it's possible that, for example, Egypt intervene in Libya and not so late. So at the moment, I think Egypt is acting any way in Libya—giving arms, weapons, money—and General Haftar has been many times in Cairo to have meetings with not only el-Sisi but all of the most important politicians of Egypt.

And so I think that it's very—Libya, it's one of the—it's the interest of Egypt at the moment and, yes, I think it's possible that they can intervene, even in an open way, not just like nowadays.

Mr. Cook. Well, I want to switch gears a little bit because we have a NATO conference coming up and some of us, both Democrats and Republicans, are part of that NATO Parliament.

And in the past, the Mediterranean members of NATO have been very, very nervous about what went on, obviously, in Tunisia and then Libya.

Now, I know that subject is going to come up. Do you have any advice on how we can handle that in terms of NATO being involved in this since they're very, very concerned about the refugee situation but also different terrorist groups just to the south of them?

Ms. Fasanotti. Well, it's difficult to answer to this question because it's—the situation is so articulated and so complex that every answer would be not enough.

But if you analyze—I think that we should start analyzing the situation right now in Cyrenaica, for example, which is strictly connected to Egypt, and in many months—not so many, Cyrenaica has now a kind of military government very similar to the el-Sisi one so which is, at the same time, different from the Tripolitania one—the GNA.

Mr. Cook. Let me jump around a little bit more because, you know, I, for one, and I think a lot of the members of the committee are very, very nervous about what's going to happen about al-Qaeda and I think it's going to be a huge target because it's oil-rich and I just—looking at a map and reading some of Churchill's commentaries on World War II at El Alamein, which is Egypt.

But the geography seems to be against the terrorists, if you will, in terms of outside allies and what have you. Can you comment on that as to how al-Qaeda, anybody, could develop there because they've obviously had a setback there, whether this will continue. Yes, sir.

Mr. Joscelyn. Well, I think the fact of the matter is, going back to 2011 we've documented both al-Qaeda and then ISIS using Libya facilitation networks to influence the situation all the way through Egypt into the Sinai—in fact, arms shipments, that kind of thing, where they've actually been able to get through, even though the Egyptian government has cracked down on a number of occasions and I will give you one stunning example.

There's a guy named Hisham al-Ashmawy who is actually a former Egyptian special forces officer who is actually one of the biggest al-Qaeda operatives in North Africa. If you meet with the Egyptians, they know, certainly, very well who Ashmawy is because he's actually targeted for assassination some senior Egyptian officials including the chief prosecutor for the Egyptian state was killed by him.

This is a very dangerous guy. He operates in Libya all the way into Egypt and, in fact, the Islamic State blames him for kicking them out of Derna because Ashmawy actually organized the jihadi resistance in Derna to the Islamic State and actually, the Islamic State put out a most wanted poster for him because they want him dead. That's how much—how dangerous he is.

So here's a guy and his network, who is both dangerous to both the Egyptian state and the Islamic State and is in fact an al-Qaeda operative. So I think that tells you quite a bit about what he's doing.

Mr. COOK. Thank you.

If you'd be so kind, if you have any background literature on that you could provide to the committee——

Mr. JOSCELYN. Sure. Absolutely.

Mr. COOK [continuing]. And we can distribute to the members.

Mr. JOSCELYN. Egyptians will know very well who he is.

Mr. COOK. Thank you very much.

All right. I'm going to turn to the ranking member, Congressman Keating, for 5 minutes.

Mr. KEATING. Thank you.

Earlier, this month General Haftar seized three oil fields—oil terminals—major oil terminals and they're just about 50 miles east of Sirte.

Now, what do you suppose—maybe Mr. Fishman could lead this—what do you suppose this might mean in terms of the peace process?

What about the signed deal to resume oil exports, in particular, in terms of these actions and do you think there's—I was in the—I was in Tunisia just a few months ago discussing things with our Libyan team and I'm just curious about what your feelings are about General Haftar, just going on—you know, going along on his own or any option about him working with us instead of independently.

I know there's a lot of questions but basically his action this month—the oil terminals—what it means in terms of the deal to resume oil exports and how does it affect the peace process and do we ever get him to somehow cooperate?

Mr. FISHMAN. Thank you. And it also relates to the—Mr. Cook's questions about Egypt because Egypt has a prominent role in influencing General Haftar.

To summarize and perhaps to simply—the greatest—the greatest asset to ridding Libya of terrorism, ISIS, al-Qaeda, whatever the threat may be, is to form a stable and unified government and that's what our administration has been trying to do for the last 3 years—plus years.

That's what the U.N.-backed process has been trying to do and that's what our major European and regional allies have been trying to do with this GNA.

The problem is with Haftar and some of his allies he's been, shall we say, the main opponent of forming a unity government because he's holding out for some high-ranking post or some regional position within that government and, obviously, the oil and the seizures of the oil fields give him more leverage to hold out further.

So in summary, Haftar is an obstacle. It's very hard to influence him. That's especially since he's made recent military progress. The problem is the Western factions—and we can go into this in more detail—are adamantly opposed to any of his contributions and the rubber meets the road where Egypt continues to support him.

And so in brief, I just—we need to find a formula through our Egyptian allies to help negotiate some kind of——

Mr. KEATING. Thank you. Mr. Joscelyn.

Mr. JOSCELYN. The question you asked, Congressman, is the one that I knew was going to be asked at this hearing and the one that I think is the trickiest one to answer for these reasons.

I actually agree with a lot of what Mr. Fishman said. I think the simple fact of the matter is that Haftar is in fact one of the key guys who has taken the fight to the jihadis in Benghazi and Derna and elsewhere.

They complain about him all the time so I know he's doing a good job with killing them, you know. Unfortunately, I think his bombing campaigns also are indiscriminate at times, you know, and you can see areas of Benghazi and elsewhere that are sort of levelled.

You know, we do see reports, too. For example, there was a helicopter that was down in Benghazi earlier this year. There were conflicting reports about whether or not it was actually shot down by the jihadis or crashed on its own accord.

Be that as it may, it confirmed that French special forces and Western special forces are also involved with him. It's not just the Egyptians but there are other Western forces that are there and so this becomes very tricky.

But by the same token, on the other side of the coin, what Mr. Fishman has outlined I think is right—that he's the political wild card and if you want a stable Libya in the future and you want to actually try and figure out a way to basically tamp down this and provide a long-term political solution for the jihadi insurgency, then he provides down side risks in that regard as well.

Mr. KEATING. Okay. I just had a quick question, having just been there.

Tunisia is extremely fragile. Could you tell me why you think, from a pro rata basis or per population member basis, that it has the highest participation in foreign terrorist fighters?

Is it economic? I've heard on the ground different theories as to why that country of all, the last remaining democratic country there, why that's so involved and so high a proportion of foreign terrorist fighters.

Mr. JOSCELYN. It's going back to the height of Iraq war. Both Tunisia and Libya on a per capita basis contributed more foreign fighters to the fight—jihadis—than basically anybody and it's a complicated story as to why.

I think radicalization, of course involves many different factors. But the bottom line is—and I wouldn't underestimate this—there is a facilitation network in Tunisia that they were able to use to send these fighters at different various facilities and, you know, some of the mosques have been radicalized and have given in to this sort of ideology, and that was a—played a major role in this.

Now, you know, just to go back to my original opening statement. Here in Tunisia is a great example of how AQIM, al-Qaeda in Islamic Maghreb and al-Qaeda play the Tunisian game.

They had group called the Uqba bin Nafi battalion, which was in fact an al-Qaeda front group—AQIM front group—that fights there.

They had some losses when it comes to the Islamic State but, again, this is another time when an organization didn't use the al-Qaeda brand name, was actually answering up the chain of authority to al-Qaeda and, you know, initially was misidentified as just a local group.

And the reason why I say that's important is because we shouldn't let them play the local game. Don't allow al-Qaeda jihadis or any jihadis to pretend that they represent Tunisian or they represent Libyans or any of them.

That's why it's important to expose them because their game is to say no, no, we represent the locals here and our—big part of our strategy has to be say, no, you don't.

Mr. KEATING. Okay. Thank you. I yield back.

Mr. COOK. Congressman Zeldin.

Mr. ZELDIN. Thank you, Mr. Chairman.

One of the many reasons why we have the greatest military in the world is our use of the after action report where we will very specifically give three sustains and three improves.

As we look back on these last few years of U.S foreign policy in Libya, whether it is tactically, operationally, strategically, if you can share what's working—specifically what's working that we need to continue and/or specifically what are we not doing that we should be or maybe what we are doing but not doing it well.

So I want to turn over my 4½ minutes to you to talk specifically about what we are doing that's working and what we are—what we need to improve upon.

Mr. JOSCELYN. Okay, I will start.

You know, I don't know if I can give you three and three but I'd say, you know, we do—we should find some encouragement in the recent military efforts in Sirte, for example. I mean, I think that that coalition that came is relying primarily on Libyan local forces from the Sirte and militiamen to take the fight to Islamic State that has worked to a large degree.

I would say there that although the local Libyan forces are doing the bulk of the fighting on the ground, I'd point you to a Washington Post article that came out recently that said, for example, the American special forces are in fact there helping them and if you look at the press reporting very carefully this is sort of the secret of Libya that I don't think is really emphasized enough.

There are probably four Western nations that have special forces footprints inside Libya today fighting. That's the U.S., the U.K., Italy, and France. And so this is very much a sort of special forces war and once you started thinking about it that way it becomes a little bit different.

I think that we've been very good at sort of, you know, recently combatting Islamic State but my big concern is in the long run how do we have something—you know, if you go back to counter insurgency in Iraq and Syria, Congressman, where you just visited in Iraq, it's clearing and then holding.

And, you know, this gain over the long run, you know, clearing is a lot easier sometimes than is holding, you know, and this is where building long-term, you know, established political institutions becomes the key thing and I don't know at this point—we've made some progress with the GNA—the Government National Accord—and others and they deserve more support. But I'm skeptical about what the long-term holds in that regard.

Mr. ZELDIN. Anybody else like to add?

Mr. FISHMAN. I think I agree with Thomas about the CT effort that has been made recently and I point back to the targeted capture operations against Abu Anas al-Libi and Abu Qatada who is responsible for the—one of the men responsible for the attack on our diplomatic facilities.

That brings up a sensitive issue because I think where we've been less successful in interacting across the region in—particularly in conflict zones is gaining access to the right people to do the right political reporting and implementing programs that these fragile governments need and that, unfortunately, has played into the politics back here but also more—there are people in the government whose careers are built in serving in conflict zones and we visited them in the military and civilian roles.

And one of our deficits in Libya particularly—you just mentioned that you visited our Libya team in Tunis. Well, they're in Tunis and they don't have access to—they have phone access to Libyans. They have access to Libyan expats. But they're not on the ground.

They're not—they're not feeling the heartbeat of Tripoli, and until we can solve this issue, I think, of getting our diplomats to find the right balance between serving in hardship and moving effectively, we are not going to be able to, I think, serve as effective interlocutors as we could.

Our European counterparts do a better job of it because they're more low profile. But, certainly, they don't have the political clout that needs to be happening.

Mr. ZELDIN. Doctor, we only have a few seconds left. Was there anything, very quickly, you wanted to add before we ran out of time?

Ms. FASANOTTI. Yes. I think we should try to understand much, much better the tribes and the internal divisions of Libya because—can I—can I go?

Mr. ZELDIN. Finish your sentence. Go ahead.

Ms. FASANOTTI. Even though it's perfectly right, the idea of controlling the terrain with military operations and so on, the problem still exists and it's a problem that exists since centuries. And now without any kind of government it's impossible to solve otherwise. So I think this.

Mr. ZELDIN. Thank you. Thank you for the extra time, Chairman.

Mr. COOK. Thank you very much.

Congressman Higgins.

Mr. HIGGINS. Well, a country of 6.5 million people, about 160 tribes, 1,600 militias, about 90 percent of the economy is oil—plummeting oil prices, no central government. What a mess. I mean, really, what—and then you have the Islamic State there as well.

These militias are made up, presumably, of—and it's a majority Sunni Muslim country. So they're probably al-Qaeda affiliates? Enlighten me.

Mr. JOSCELYN. I mean, the—the al-Qaeda groups are—you can distinguish them from the vast majority of the militias. The militias a lot of times—and this is where I objected to some of the al-Qaeda groups being called militias back in 2011 and 2012 because they weren't.

You know, they were—they were very insidious. No, there are a lot of militias that do local security work, which is what you're talking about, which are a much more local power base and this is where Libya is a fractured society, as the doctor said.

Mr. HIGGINS. Wait a minute. How do you—how do you distinguish between what militias do in Syria, for example, and militias that are a local security group?

Mr. JOSCELYN. Well, no. This is—this is part of the challenge, absolutely. But I would say this. What I'd say is of the—I think 1,600 is the number you used, something along those lines.

Mr. HIGGINS. That's what——

Mr. JOSCELYN. Right. Somewhere along those lines. We—I mean, obviously, we don't have perfect information on Libya. I'm not claiming I do.

But we track it very carefully and I can tell you that, you know, we don't see—you know, the vast majority of those militias as far as we can tell from open source information appear to be sort of local security groups. They're not involved in sort of the jihadi insurgency activities.

Now, Congressman, to your point, however, you know, going back through time, some of the militias did get entangled with Ansar al-Sharia and others and that's where it became complex in Benghazi and elsewhere.

But, you know, I think if you'd taken that 1,600 number, my guess is, and it's an informed guess, most of those are local security forces.

Mr. HIGGINS. Okay. But it's still a country of only 6.5 million people so it's relatively small. It is—you don't have a Shi'a-Sunni divide as you have in Syria, as you have in Iraq, because 97 percent are Sunni Muslims.

What are the dividing lines? These tribes or——

Ms. FASANOTTI. It's—can I? It's a question of history and ancient times, and of course, the tribes are still—if you—if we analyze the tribes one century ago, we can see that they are still in the same place of the 1926, for example, and the frictions of those tribes are still the same because, for example, Misrata, which is a tribe of the

Tripolitania, and Zintan, which everyone knows because Zintan militias, they are still fighting. So nothing has changed in this way.

Mr. HIGGINS. Who finances the militias?

Ms. FASANOTTI. Sorry?

Mr. HIGGINS. Who finances the militias?

Ms. FASANOTTI. Some—many, in many ways. They can fi- nance——

Mr. HIGGINS. They, presumably, tax the people over which they are providing security for?

Ms. FASANOTTI. Maybe. Yes.

Mr. HIGGINS. So that's a source of revenue?

Ms. FASANOTTI. Yes.

Mr. FISHMAN. Actually, I don't mean to interrupt but——

Mr. HIGGINS. Jump in.

Mr. FISHMAN [continuing]. Many of them are financed from the state itself and that's the paradox of how to solve this problem because after the——

Mr. HIGGINS. Solve the problem to what end?

Mr. FISHMAN. Getting the militias to form up in a coherent security service that answer to a state authority and instead this is called DDR, Defense, Deconstruction—or Demobilization, Disarmament, and Reconstruction—sorry—and it's a common process in counter insurgency and it just hasn't taken off in Libya in part because there were poor decisions early on by the Libyan government to incorporate the militias as, basically, state actors, and all the while they are earning their salaries effectively holding the state hostage to persist in this—the civil war.

And so you're—I just want to make one more point about your Islamist association with the militias. The civil war was initiated by a large faction that's pro-Islamist and a large faction that's anti-Islamist.

It's implying things but in general and so I don't know whether the percentage is 50/50, 60/40, 70/30, whatever. But a lot of those militias reject the premise of Islamists and those primarily are the ones who helped kick out ISIS from Sirte.

Mr. HIGGINS. Thank you, Mr. Chairman.

Mr. COOK. Thank you. Congressman Perry.

Mr. PERRY. Thanks, Mr. Chairman.

Mr. Fishman, you're—are you with RAND now?

Mr. FISHMAN. I'm an adjunct there so I'm not officially part of the organization. I just help them with various projects.

Mr. PERRY. Okay. And before doing that, you were at—were you at State?

Mr. FISHMAN. I was at the International Institute for Strategic Studies.

Mr. PERRY. Okay. And before that State?

Mr. FISHMAN. The NSC at the White House, then at State.

Mr. PERRY. Okay. And before that?

Mr. FISHMAN. State.

Mr. PERRY. What's that?

Mr. FISHMAN. State Department.

Mr. PERRY. Before that State Department.

Mr. FISHMAN. Mm-hmm.

Mr. PERRY. How—when did you start at the State?

Mr. FISHMAN. 2009.

Mr. PERRY. 2009. Before that?

Mr. FISHMAN. I was in graduate school at Washington Institute for Near East Policy.

Mr. PERRY. Okay. So I'm looking through your submission here and it says misrepresentation one—we should never have gone into Libya in the first place. The threat was not significant to the U.S. or the Libyan population. Gaddafi could have been placated. That's misrepresentation one, right?

Mr. FISHMAN. That's what I submitted.

Mr. PERRY. And then misrepresentation two—NATO and the U.S. abandoned Libya after the intervention. There should have been a stabilization force assembled to restore security. That's two, correct?

Mr. FISHMAN. Correct.

Mr. PERRY. Makes it easier. So just out of curiosity, what was your position regarding the United States intervention, if you want to call it that, in Iraq?

Mr. FISHMAN. In Iraq?

Mr. PERRY. Yes.

Mr. FISHMAN. You mean in 2003?

Mr. PERRY. Yes.

Mr. FISHMAN. I was—contemporaneously I was supportive of the intervention in Iraq.

Mr. PERRY. I'm sorry. I didn't—you what?

Mr. FISHMAN. I supported it as a college student.

Mr. PERRY. You supported the intervention in Iraq?

Mr. FISHMAN. Yes.

Mr. PERRY. Okay. And so you're supporting the intervention in Libya because you're saying that there's a misrepresentation. We should have never gone into Libya in the first place.

But I'm wondering if there was a plan post-Gaddafi—if there was a plan for governance at State, at the National Security Council for the follow-on operation in Libya once Gaddafi was gone.

Mr. FISHMAN. There were many, many discussions at both an agency level, interagency level, international level about how to help stabilize the Libyans.

Mr. PERRY. But was there a plan? Not just a discussion but was there a plan? This is, what, 2000—this—essentially the overthrow of Gaddafi occurred fall of 2011, right?

Mr. FISHMAN. Yes.

Mr. PERRY. So it had been going on——

Mr. FISHMAN. Yes.

Mr. PERRY [continuing]. It had been leading up to that for some time but was there a—and we were involved and——

Mr. FISHMAN. We had stabilization planning documents and the nature of the fall of the regime led to the fact that those plans had to change on the fly.

Mr. PERRY. Were you—were you privy to those plans?

Mr. FISHMAN. Some, but not all of them.

Mr. PERRY. So are you familiar with Presidential Study Directive 11?

Mr. FISHMAN. You have to remind me.

42

Mr. PERRY. Okay. So it's a classified document. You can find some open source information. I'm happy to provide what we know for you.

But it's essentially changing decades of United States policy in favour of authoritarian rulers such as Gaddafi for the sake of stability in the region in North Africa and the Middle East and partnering with the—with the local population in overthrowing those governments in—for the sake of democracy and partnering specifically with the Muslim Brotherhood in that effort.

Are you familiar with that? Did that play into your——

Mr. FISHMAN. I don't recall any such directive and I recall a similar study about supporting reform in the region. But it was certainly——

Mr. PERRY. Well, what drove who you partnered with or who you worked with? What determined that effort? How was that defined for you?

Mr. FISHMAN. In the Libya circumstance?

Mr. PERRY. Sure. Libya is one of—by the way, one of the target countries in Presidential Study Directive 11—Libya, Syria, Yemen, Egypt. All the failed ones are delineated and specifically named, according to open source.

Mr. FISHMAN. I think that your—if I recall correctly, and it was several years ago, that document referred to how we can support gradual change for institutional reform in countries that you named who we thought assessed to be long-term threats to stability if you—if the authoritarian regimes continued as they were.

And you saw as a result we didn't push—we didn't push Tunisia to rid themselves with Ben Ali. The Ben Ali regime portrayed it that those offenses——

Mr. PERRY. I'm sorry, sir. My time has expired. Thank you, Mr. Chairman.

Mr. COOK. Thank you very much.

Congresswoman Kelly.

Ms. KELLY. Doctor, in your statement you discuss restructuring the Libyan armed forces, national security forces and local police.

How do you envision countries like the United States or other outside actors assisting in this effort without—I know there was a comment we do have special forces there without committing more and more and more troops. What military ideas do you have?

Ms. FASANOTTI. Well, I—still, I don't have any clear idea of this. Mine is just a suggestion, knowing the country, and so of course, in my opinion we should intervene in a more systematic way because you cannot—I think that security, like economy and politics, are profoundly restricted to the other.

So I think that we have to invest, first of all, as I was telling before, in the security, of course, because if you don't have security you cannot work.

But on the other side, we have to invest even in all these incredible divisions that Libya has because Libya is not only what we talk right now about or we said about Islamist, non-Islamist, militias, different militias, militias in Tripoli, militias in Benghazi, in Derna and so on. But there are the tribes and then there are diversity at an ethnic level.

So Arabs—because we talk about Shi'a and Sunni but here we have atavistic divisions in terms of ethnicities. So Arabs were the Bedouins and Berbers, Tuareg, Amazigh, and Toubou.

So in this way, I think, yes, of course we should invest in the disarming, for example, because we cannot have, frankly, 6 million people and almost at minimum 20 million weapons.

Ms. KELLY. Do you think outside forces, depending on who it is, would further divide Libya? Because you talk about all the tribes and the different groups already. Do you think it's the United States that should intervene or——

Ms. FASANOTTI. This is a very difficult answer because Libyans are really particular, even in this way, because they do not want to be touched by anyone.

They want, of course, to decide for themselves and I can understand them, of course. And so all—what I see is that all this continues in interventions open or—not opened by the international community. At the moment, did not obtain anything. So——

Ms. KELLY. Welcome to jump in.

Mr. JOSCELYN. Oh, geez. This is a very complex question. I don't know—I don't have all the answers. I will just say this.

The—on the other side of the coin, when you talk about Western intervention or assistance, I will tell you what the al-Qaeda jihadis are doing, which is that they're organizing themselves against that.

And so what they in their propaganda, and we've seen this as a major theme, they're holding up Omar Al-Mukhtar, who was—in the first half of the 20th century resisted Italian, you know, forces in Italy.

Ms. FASANOTTI. Yes, a hero.

Mr. JOSCELYN. Yes, hero. What's happening now is, and I see this in the videos—I see this in the magazines that they put out in Arabic and in different languages—al-Qaeda is trying to portray him as sort of this ancestor of theirs in Libya and they're trying to rally forces around his image to say that they're also resisting sort of Western interference.

So, for example, when this French—this helicopter carrying three French special forces officers went down in Benghazi earlier this year, immediately that became a flashpoint where the so-called Grand Mufti of Libya—he's not really but that's how he—what he's called—immediately comes out and says this proves that France and the West is intervening here in Libya and we need to rally our forces on the jihadi and Islamist side against any outside interference.

And so it's a complex dynamic. That's only one factor, of course, in all of this. But I can tell you that there are people on the other side thinking about that and never to forget that.

Mr. FISHMAN. Just in 2 seconds—that's why our planning, as well as it was done, ran into easy or specific opposition by the interim leaders, as I noted at the beginning, whether it was on security issues or economic issues, and legally you can't deploy troops for security reasons.

You can't deploy technical assistance if the government doesn't sign an agreement and much like the Iraq issue with the withdrawal of our troops, we didn't have agreement from the Libyans.

Ms. KELLY. I yield back, Mr. Chair.

Mr. COOK. Thank you very much.

What I want to do is thank the panellists for being here today. I want to thank the members and just want to also second my prayers and thoughts are with Judge Poe, the chairman, and hope that he gets better.

And I want to thank the member from Buffalo and the one from Massachusetts for being civil today toward each other, knowing that there's a big game at stake. Counsellors are standing by and I've given them a copy of Kumbaya, which they will memorize before the next hearing.

But I do want to thank everybody, and right now this subcommittee is adjourned. Thank you.

[Whereupon, at 3:54 p.m., the subcommittee was adjourned.]

APPENDIX

<small>MATERIAL SUBMITTED FOR THE RECORD</small>

SUBCOMMITTEE HEARING NOTICE
COMMITTEE ON FOREIGN AFFAIRS
U.S. HOUSE OF REPRESENTATIVES
WASHINGTON, DC 20515-6128

Subcommittee on Terrorism, Nonproliferation, and Trade
Ted Poe (R-TX), Chairman

TO: MEMBERS OF THE COMMITTEE ON FOREIGN AFFAIRS

You are respectfully requested to attend an OPEN hearing of the Committee on Foreign Affairs, to be held by the Subcommittee on Terrorism, Nonproliferation, in Room 2200 of the Rayburn House Office Building (and available live on the Committee website at http://www.ForeignAffairs.house.gov):

DATE: Tuesday, September 27, 2016

TIME: 2:15 p.m.

SUBJECT: Libya's Terrorist Descent: Causes and Solutions

WITNESSES: Federica Saini Fasanotti, Ph.D.
Non-Resident Fellow
Center for 21st Century Security and Intelligence
Foreign Policy Program
The Brookings Institution

Mr. Thomas Joscelyn
Senior Editor
Long War Journal
Foundation for Defense of Democracies

Mr. Benjamin Fishman
(Former Director for North Africa, National Security Council)

By Direction of the Chairman

The Committee on Foreign Affairs seeks to make its facilities accessible to persons with disabilities. If you are in need of special accommodations, please call 202/225-5021 at least four business days in advance of the event, whenever practicable. Questions with regard to special accommodations in general (including availability of Committee materials in alternative formats and assistive listening devices) may be directed to the Committee.

47

COMMITTEE ON FOREIGN AFFAIRS

MINUTES OF SUBCOMMITTEE ON _____ *Terrorism, Nonproliferation, and Trade* _____ HEARING

Day___ *Tuesday* ___ Date___ *September 27, 2016* ___ Room_____ *2200* _____

Starting Time ___ *2:47 p.m.* ___ Ending Time ___ *3:54 p.m.* ___

Recesses |_____| (____to ____) (____to ____) (____to ____) (____to ____) (____to ____) (____to ____)

Presiding Member(s)

Rep. Paul Cook

Check all of the following that apply:

Open Session ☑
Executive (closed) Session ☐
Televised ☑

Electronically Recorded (taped) ☑
Stenographic Record ☑

TITLE OF HEARING:

"Libya's Terrorist Descent: Causes and Solutions"

SUBCOMMITTEE MEMBERS PRESENT:

Reps. Cook, Keating, Wilson, Higgins, Perry, Castro, Zeldin, Kelly

NON-SUBCOMMITTEE MEMBERS PRESENT: *(Mark with an * if they are not members of full committee.)*

HEARING WITNESSES: Same as meeting notice attached? Yes ☑ No ☐
(If "no", please list below and include title, agency, department, or organization.)

STATEMENTS FOR THE RECORD: *(List any statements submitted for the record.)*

TIME SCHEDULED TO RECONVENE _____
or
TIME ADJOURNED ___ *3:54 p.m.* ___

Subcommittee Staff Associate